SPIRITED WORDS
(Embellished potpourri of verses)
Mensah Louis Joel
+233245802472

Table of contents
1. Disguised Assassin
2. A Pig in a Pork
3. Tears in My Eyes
4. Abandoned Sheep
5. The Fate Prominent Men Share
5. Society's Eminent Enemies
6. The Anguish of Dire Poverty
7. Alcohol - A Saboteur
8. God Cares
9. What Is Wrong with Our World
10. Be Kind
11. Every City ; Once a Village
12. Man Toils- Why?
13. Sealed by Nature- No Alteration
14. All Shall Die
15. Children of One
16. What I Am
17. Woes of Abortion
18. Don't Be Lazy
19. Exuding Love
20. Alone Aside
21. He Exists Not
22. That's Its Way
23. Unparallelism

DISGUISED ASSASSIN
'Twas glowing magic.
The heart quakes but affirms.
Affirmation was for one angelic.
One that it often confirms.

A grin tore a space in the heart.
'Twas a path for the spirit entry.
There was a pat.
This was no flattery.

With a storm its euphoria it quenched
And traces it did bury.
Nothing with it matched
It is unbridled fury.

A PIG IN A PORK
(Poetic autobiography)

I loved a pig in a pork . . .
She was by my side always,
Her beauty so seraphic,
 made me salivated.

No second passed, and my soul
was whole, in her absence.
Our affinity grew wilder
It reached its climax!

I relished seeing an angel
Beside me.
Her vivid memory never
left me

A swizz climbed onto our faces
when something should prevent our entwining

Sultriness and coquetry
seethed in the walls
of her flesh
Her wanton eyes
Her soothing speeches
Enamored me; yet innocence
shielded me from the facts
behind the designer's wear

Oh innocence !
You shield colossus of mischief .
Realized ones made me a petrified
Egyptian mummy
Sultry coquettish exposure umpteenly
unraveled before my naked eyes secretly .
I indolently watched but
comprehension; o my comprehension!
was far away.

Her soul quivers for illegitimate
loving
She straddled me tightly while
We're behind telly and book
The imbecile did not abscond to
save his Acadian life when he expected
his "light" to blaze, ceaselessly.

My nights were marred by hallucinations,
dreams I call them.
They often tore me from strong arms
of Morpheus
 where I was deep in somnolence.
Such thoughts crammed my mind.
 Compelled emotions made me nurse
amorosity;
 I made it nestle, on my chest .

Our joy excelled to the heavens,

even euphoria was lower.
She is not imposting I say!
She never ceased to remind me to
do the "dailies".
She also agreed to be in my company at fellowship.
Time failed to grant her wish!

My eyes were dim but I relished
Soaring in love, far into the sky
like an April gentleman.
No persuasion however worked to
clarify what was happening
behind the walls to me.

We cooed and billed.
I preened myself from the unripe
meat forced down my throat.

She explored all grounds where a
psychologist, a stubborn and adamant
attorney will fail to know
his position and with alacrity
succumb, but no
response from the Egyptian Mummy.
Not even a sensational
part was nudged

Knowledge has finished.
She thumped her palm for accepting
defeat over all her knowledge.
It was an anathema, no being loves defeat
I hardly accept one.

The love and care metamorphosed
into hatred which oozed abruptly.

Melody! Her lovely name.
An instrument of joy that was
Ungratifying to my soul.
Parted for months, I was

still innocent over the whole show.
with queries I went in.
The only response which emanated
between her naturally red
and miniature lips was:

"You did not offend me in any way"
Persuasion of no kind was able
to coax my "black angel" to
To clear my mind.
She is a fair mesmerizing
lady, I say.

I bought a pig in a pork,
I realized
the calibre she was made of, veiled
behind bashful smiles.
Game Phase II was on the field
Unprepared, I spot my lady.
She has anger in her formerly
lovely eyes.
Eyes over which I heaved relief.

Hard questions, were
pouring from my head as I racked
my brain to squeeze out all
that was requisite to evacuate
the ordeal traumatizing me.

All efforts landed on
rocky ground and
only cleaned the hardened rock.
Despair, finally
sang victory over my groaning soul.

I felt some glee when the chance of
change of environment popped up
I laid calm for the D-day of departure
to come by so that I can dash out.

She heard the circulating news
She doubted its truthfulness.
Sooner, she knew it is the end

She tried to soothe my soul
O no! the time has passed
the environ has changed
I was in good mood to
understand that "to err is human"
Faulty approach!
Every secret come to light
It started:
I forgive you . . .

That letter
landed in the hands of a guardian who
had iron hands to scarthe
nothing made sense
scolding my angel

fueled the dying trouble.
I bolted.
Info about facing the music
reached me.
My hands were clean!

In amazement, everything frizzled out .

Persuaded she consent to chat me .
This we did for
the sixtieth of an hour.
Reminiscence of our cherished love
made me love sick after parting.

TEARS IN MY EYES
Young and faithful was our love.
All days, at all times.
We clanged to each other
As birds of a feather do.
Conversations we had secluded,
sitting on a mould of cloud:
 only both of us.
All other human beings were beasts.

We wedded each other at last!
Our faces beamed
With unprecedented joy.
We salivated as if
We were ready to lick a full
Ice cream to the bottom in a second
In the pool of love
We've drawn.

Days and passing years posed no danger
To our cherished love!
Amicably, we solved our misunderstandings.
Love, some are hearts.
Others , stones .
'Tis true!

That day ... my immortal memory...
You yelled at me
Ruthlessly , you pounced on me.
You're a human
You'd not feel for me.
Our love became past tense.

Tears clouded my eyes and streamed down it
What wrong have I done?
I became an opponent in a ring.

Are these the vows of the vivid nights?
Nobody best understands
The heat of the sunny afternoon ...
It burnt me .

My body, o my poor body!
I shall never forget that day!
Is this the end of our love?

ABANDONED SHEEP

Oh my love.
I missed you!
Your cheeks that beamed.
Your lips between which broke
Live smiles, just vanished.

Oh my love!
You've left me in the rain!
Th dark clouds scudding the troubled sky,
Stabbed my heart.
With a sword of Damocles.
How it roared over it...
Terribly, like a hungry lion,
Seeking, a prey!

The torrent started!
I had no shelter,
Very poor was me.
I was exposed to the sheet .
I was an abandoned sheep.

The torrent weakened my poor body
I sighed and trembled

At the touch of the cold wind
It went through my bones

Where were you, my love?
The life of my life,
I need you.

THE FATE PROMINENT MEN SHARE
A prominent man
Is insignificant at inception.
Alas! He still murmuring lips

His toil and magnificent goal,
Required massive labour.
Sometimes it is mitigated
By "reason" seekers.

He presses on,
He has one target
The zenith alone!
Disappointment tends to veer,
topple or swivel him .
He persists still he breaks the
Shell of his vision.

They pursue their ambitions.
Solitarily in secrets .
Very determined, they burn
Their candles through the dark night.
They're tagged "time wasters ".
They create the cherished picture.
Dream "in there" !
Long to see it materialise !

In all his toil and combat
With the challenge on his way
He springs out with a crux –
"I shall one day become a figure
I want admiration from all"

Words intended to coax,
Do not tear him from his goal.
Lo and behold! His good becomes better.
He achieves that aim in great joy.

SOCIETY'S EMINENT ENEMIES
Late in the dark night
That's their work place
In the lonely peaceful land,
their souls cherish evil and stab men
ruthlessly, with wants

Good is to them anathema.
Evil is their ambition for life.
That, that dark night, they reason about
how to make sons of men lose something.
They sneak to coffers.
Evil laden are they.
Mercy for mankind is not nominated
in their boiling brain.
They live in affluence briefly
They endeavour to satisfy
their burning desire
with alacrity

Their eyes are fixed on any gem,
They think of the void means of acquisition
Their lives are short
Advocates of the law shoot them.

Their ambition is no fair aspiration.
Their love for the "dirty'" profession
Makes them direct enemies of constables
and the entire society.
All they do is to hurt us
So we hate them.

THE ANGUISH OF DIRE POVERTY
Poverty so dire frightens the rich.
It is the poor's coffers.
The destined struggle with it all his life
To no avail

The rich becomes miserly
The intent in terse is
'I may become an underdog'
They monitor the movement of even pennies.

Some poors choose dubious means
To acquire riches
To escape poverty
This yields them a trouble – packed life

They visit the occultists
To expurgate the stench
From their lives entirely.
Wages of duping hastelessly meet them

Couples may part for poverty
Consenting to it glumly style lives
They detest that destiny.
Mismanagement welcomes poverty
 A fool and his money are soon parted

Poverty stripes men of dignity
With his "martel" he breaks homes
 Some become preoccupied thinkers.

Many lives are thwarted under this theme.
"I don't have ... "
They could not pay hospital bills, or rent.

Some people desirous of the top of the ladder of success,
"mark time" at its foot
Despite requisite qualifications
Some struggle hard at it. Others give up

Poverty makes some
Captors of those who,
Like captives seek help from them
It muddles their lives.

ALCOHOL A SABOTEUR
Liquid of liquids!
"Terrible terror' is your pseudonym.
In your name are the nations gone mad
Poverty and wailing are your children
You are named King of drinks.
Man pursues you with voracity

Your captive stagger and wobble
To their utmost discomfort
You cunningly assault them.
They never see the anger
Scribbled on your grimace.
Blood on your reddened eyes they see
As normal even on your feigning face.

Your advocates are indirect assailants,
They are grave diggers
 Dipsomania is your gift
Some people are unfilled after numerous stings.

Your children increase,
Parents are left destitute.
For your wickedness
Marriages cease to bind
Easily got too, you are exceedingly
A jeopardy to the human race

You quake your prey irately,
You leave them to stagger, ending in gutters
In discomfort
Disgrace thou art really to the race.

GOD CARES
Life in man
Is held in the hands of a power so caring
No matter how storms pummel on a boat
God cares
He stills them to your utter dismay

When everything is absolutely wrong
There is someone who stretches
His hands to the human race.
He whispers solemn and soothing words.
It turns the anguish of a troubled heart.
"Peace be still" He says

The world: its kingdoms and nations,
Shout at one another irately.
They tend to ravage entirely
 any captive found.
A voice from the heavens
Descends into the human heart to tell 'em
"Please do not fight, for you're brethr'n"

The orphans, the widows, the waifs and immigrants
Seek filial love, good caring and safe journey.
Though He's never seen
His hands of mercy never cease to provide
all needs even abundantly.

He who promises
The human generation protection
Never slumbers.
He stretches his agile hands over man.
He ensures him comfort in the dark night
No matter how the waves roar furiously
Quaking the ground under your feet,
With his power, he strengthens your feet

While the sun hotly burns
And man terribly thirsts,
He opens the waters to all men:
He cares so much about all

The hands of that Merciful one weave the future.
He plans it
That man should end up
Enjoying the fruit of his labour
God cares no matter what
If the whole world disgusts you;
And wish to hush your voice in cold blood
He will come to your rescue
In all things ... God cares!

WHAT IS WRONG WITH OUR WORLD
It's astonishing to describe the wonders
our generation imbibes.
The pen of man could hardly
Transform them onto paper
 fully described

What is wrong with the youth of today?
Indecent dressing is ignorantly quoted "fashion"
Is it thrilling to dress normally
with trews sliding the buttocks?
 This they continually pull
as if dipsomaniac, very distorted.

With th same temerity lasses dress as if call girls
Leggers, mini skirts and dresses
They reveal the image of their naked body
Under one mind – "fashion"

They gyrate gleefully to any form of song devoid of sense
In the name of music
Advice is fading away for
Vulgar words in music today.

Immorality rockets amidst the youth;
This seems to be the marriage they admire.
Those who are adamant to erotic dresses
Are humorously nicknamed "john"

Eeriness to the elders of yesterday!

Aged men and woman take their children and grandchildren
As their spouses.
The captives involved
Call their arcane captors
"sugar mummies and daddies"
Sissies become wives and tomboys husband to their sex mates.

Nature is not pleased with this.
It yields them a curse they would not understand
You could hear of rape everywhere.
Robbery and duping is soaring
Hermaphrodites and monsters
Multiplying in our generation

The cause of all these remains a mystery
Things beyond the credibility of man
Is what our generation embraces
What at all is wrong
With the world of today?

BE KIND
Be kind to all especially
The pauper and the disabled –
They need a share of your joy
To make their life scintillating

Kindness is a Christian ethic
It is Zakat – the pillar of Islam,
Every other religion
Promulgate kindness in their teachings
Even secularists do not forget it.

As taught by the aphorism of nature
"Kindness is reciprocated to whoever its due"
Thus we all need be

It saves in times of jeopardy

Scrooges and the wicked shall not find
the least favour in the eyes of anybody
in their troubled times
They lived not being kind
To see good, flamboyant and colourful days
be kind

EVERY CITY ONCE A VILLAGE
The sky scrapers in the Western World,
The edifice of nations;
The mansions countries have,
So mesmerizing,
Are built by men of higher
architectural minds
These neither existed in a day
nor were conjured in a second
The inceptions were villages!
Through purposed periods
Buildings are fabulously flying
Into the sky

"Let not the coal call the kettle black"
For thy are all of the same category:

Cities evolved from villages
Villages from cottages.
Let there be respect to all
Irrespective of their abode

Science, Math and
Profound learning styles . . .
The mind of man was not at its
Zenith for him to think of mightier,
Stronger and embellished buildings
In the former era

The inception of every city
Is a village

MAN TOILS – WHY?
"No cross, no crown"
So the adage goes
Not being in the race is exempted.
All toil irrespective of
Age, race and condition
Food, peace, love and power:
All are toil got
Man from his inception had
toiling a destiny.
He ought to toil to fill
The stomach and must
Likewise clothe himself
Nothing so genuine is easy in
This world.

SEALED BY NATURE – NO ALTERATION
Nature made it so thus man is stilled
There is no power in the tongue of man
to alter any decision of nature
His will all being succumb to
without questioning
Nature chooses destiny for
the human race
and they all act accordingly.
"Tis the will of nature that there is
variation in humans, animals and plants.
She abases and exalts.
Nature to thy holy name all nations
ought to hail praises
Your deed is beyond
the little minded "homo sapien"
We are speechless at your deeds

ALL SHALL DIE
"Dust you are; into dust you shall return"
All irrespective of age, colour
structure, wealth and position
go into this humble earth.
She is ready to receive
her beloved children back
to herself.
Man aspires higher
He wishes to him all
Other beings; animals and birds
Sing songs in glory.
Man is never gratified with the little
He spontaneously got.
He says "I wish I were the God of the Earth"

In all this toil , he endeavours not
to prepare his soul for death
He knocks on man's door in innocence.
"The end of everything is better
than the beginning"
Says the preacher.

Man knows not when death with
unpardoning "martel" raised so high
will reach his door; grinning impishly
and tell "I'm here. . . tis your turn!
There is no power in
the tongue of man to alter it.

CHILDREN OF ONE
Equally we are made.
One is the creator of all of us
Man, O man! Why segregate?

You're born
with a silver spoon
in your mouth
I am born

on a tattered piece of cloth,
thus segregate?
You are beautiful
I am ugly
You are black
I am white
At death we bear one name – corpse

Your beauty and
My ugliness?
They await decay
Our wealth shall be left here.
When death calls us.

Nobody precisely knows
morrow
What is the future like?

The hands of the Merciful one
weave the future
Who knows
whether the rich will also
become a pauper
or the pauper will become wealthy?

The world is split – level
and changes at will.
Do not swagger today forgetting morrow
could be a quimpering time.
No matter how seraphic you are,
you are below perfection

No matter how ugly and horrific
you look,
there is a gift of nature
very attractive and unique in you.

Children of one,
let your father's work
be equally pleasant

in your eyes
Do not segregate.

WHAT I AM
I am so small
I am so thin
I am so little
Yet I am very important
Many people posses me
I am mightier than
the gadget for battle;
especially: the sword
There is no written literature
in my absence
I am a weapon to a tutor.
Like arrows in the quiver of the archer
so I am to him.
Those in grade school
Use my spilt blood in their work

Unscrupulous clerks
misuse my precious blood
to my aversion
How I hate to see them pilfer with me

I am proud to make all
recognise my preeminence

WOES OF ABOTRTION
The "silent scream"
That is all it takes to damage the dream
Enjoyment at all cost. Sure!
The human race goes extinct: Sure!
Facing the consequence of relish
Squarely you shrieked at . Sure!

Prominent lives are lost
Poignantly:

The most pessimistic mannerism in
inhuman humans – abortion!

"Rescue the perishing,
care for the dying
The hymnal irrefutably affirms

Women! Women!
Women are said to be
the most sympathetic
and most humane of all humans . . .
Yet,

At par with the majority
some are malignate and sense devoid:
Killing the prospective holders of
the future generation
mattes less to them.

Doctors: savers of lives"
Wield knives that stab and remove,
The innocent foetus
Which lay calm in the womb,
Anticipating emancipation!

They fuel and advocate
The removal of
Unwanted fertilized eggs.
How ruthless! The act is inhuman!

Increase and replenish the earth
faces mortification
Every evil shall surely be paid.

DON'T BE LAZY
Stand up and fast.
Do you want to be down
and become the last
to get up early in the dawn?

The rain was early in the season.
The sluggish never gets it.
Having laid dearly and led the farewell.
The door to sorrow is opened wide
Beds made are left with
No seed on them.

The ground to dig,
on the hill by its sides
was a tedious task
seeds are sown
so unfailing were the rains
like wind that had blown
which did no harm to the drains

Yields of crop from toil,
Blessed are in the soil.
Given by all fields to all that
Labour unfailingly

EXUDING LOVE
Swiftly flying it came across it.
Coming with grains spread
on the dry ground.
From love and pure heart,
it left them for it to get all and alone.

It flies back all day knowing
sweet awaits it somewhere.
Supplying that is its joy.

Paths came face – to – face,

The day's today, thought Bird.
Mustered courage, it waited yet prepared to
defend to th latter if a jeopardy crops – up

Friendship is all I want . . .
a lucid enunciation of the quadruped.
Abruptly its heart stopped to heave.
The green – a sign of fruitfulness.
They coalesced easily

The bird thinks it was not a problem
The other can't fly, it was so vice versa
Compromising and complying with one
another's ways, friendship unbreakable
thrives ever and ever.

ALONE ASIDE
Near the countryside,
That is where I reside.
Over there I decide,
To in the end be aside.
Nothing makes me feel to be inside
The group reaches not the country side
I love to be alone on the side.

HE EXISTS NOT
The world, its kingdoms
and nations, as mighty as they are
- United?
They contribute towards
the repudiation of the Almighty.

They pull His dignity from
His hands in the face of
fellow men.
The Almighty is left with rage.
He swallows it with equanimity

The collusion of the generation
Become clear to His aged but agile mind.
Human with his power
explores heaven and earth
with alacrity looking for
His physical existence.

"No sign of feasibility"
they say with gratification – '
There is no God.
Jews, Christians, Muslims others cite Him
Only for to regard a body mightier
Than the human
To whom all must bow sheepishly

The God of the earth liveth.
His power,
will soon show.
The face of man of the earth
will be turned pale.
Their lips will cease
to utter
any word.

THAT'S ITS WAY
It is a flame.
It blazes when fuelled.
Nurturing a baby has something
in common with the flame –
Nursing a seed is its best description.

It assails the heart of humans
It is veiled from mortal eyes.
It is fathomless when thought of
The assailant is cunning:
It averts thoughts averse to it.

It is an irresistible power.

None in the rational race
Falls in its pool looking for its
Survival refuses to succumb.
Irrespective of the pummelling storm,
They hope for peace at the shore.

It leads a lot into utopia.
Living in euphoria is embraced.
Nobody feels its seething
Only the captured knows well
How it feels like.
"you'll not understand" they always say.

UNPARALLELISM
Ugh! It feels like a pain.
Bitterness rose into my throat
Having blue – blood in one's veins,
is no mystery immortalized.
Blessed is the initiator of nobility?

Greener pasture is fed to fatty cattle.
Honey drips onto few tongues
Blessed be the goose that lays eggs of gold.
The man seldom covered, showed his
Only cloth left.
The sun stared at his skin and makes it frail.
Glumly lay he prostrate.
Reluctantly saluted he the mighty –

In blue – blood there is a sprawl,
struggle is coffers to who's striped of glory
the immortal lane is seldom trodden
it could be invisible to his eyes forever.

NB:
"Martel" is the Latin for hammer.

www.ingramcontent.com/pod-product-compliance
Lightning Source LLC
Chambersburg PA
CBHW031601210526
45464CB00003B/1381